Governments
Around the World

David Scott

Consultants

William O'Mara, Ph.D.
History Professor
California State University, Dominguez Hills

Jon Anger
English, History, and ELD Teacher
Novato Unified School District

Publishing Credits

Rachelle Cracchiolo, M.S.Ed., *Publisher*
Emily R. Smith, M.A.Ed., *SVP of Content Development*
Véronique Bos, *Vice President of Creative*
Dani Neiley, *Editor*
Fabiola Sepulveda, *Series Graphic Designer*

Image Credits: p.7 Photo © Zev Radovan/Bridgeman Images; p.8 (top) Lebrecht History/ Bridgeman Images; p.8 (bottom) Peter Newark Western Americana/Bridgeman Images; p.9 Alamy/PA Images; p.10 (top) Shutterstock/ImageArc; p.10 (bottom) U.S. Department of State; p.11 (top) Alamy/Everett Collection Historical/Alamy Stock Photo; p.11 (bottom) Alamy/Aflo Co. Ltd.; p.13 (bottom) Alamy/Couvrette/Ottawa (613) 238-5104 www. couvrette-photography.on.ca; p.14 © NPL–DeA Picture Library/Bridgeman Images; p.15 (top) Ministry of Information Photo Division Photographer; p.15 (bottom) Wikimedia/ Popolon; p.17 (top) Alamy/UPI; p.18 (top) Auckland War Memorial Museum; p.18 (bottom) Alamy/PA Images; p.19 (top) Alamy/2020 Images; p.20 (top) © Look and Learn/Bridgeman Images; p.20 (bottom) Shutterstock/Claire Whitehead; p.21 (top) Shutterstock/Lev Radin; p.22 (top) Shutterstock/Grebeshkovmaxim; p.22 (center) iStock/Stacey Newman; p.25 (center) Alamy/Benedicte Desrus; p.26 Alamy/American Photo Archive; all other images from iStock and/or Shutterstock

Library of Congress Cataloging-in-Publication Data

Names: Scott, David (David Coleman), 1971- author.
Title: Governments around the world / David Scott.
Description: Huntington Beach, CA : Teacher Created Materials, Inc, [2023]
| Includes index. | Audience: Ages 8-18 | Summary: "Governments were
created long ago when civilizations began. But in modern times,
governments have become more complex. Society is organized by
governments. There are local, state, and national governments. They are
different around the world. But they all work to protect and serve their
citizens"-- Provided by publisher.
Identifiers: LCCN 2022038395 (print) | LCCN 2022038396 (ebook) | ISBN
9781087695228 (paperback) | ISBN 9781087695389 (ebook)
Subjects: LCSH: Political science--History--Juvenile literature. |
Political leadership--History--Juvenile literature.
Classification: LCC JA70 .S36 2023 (print) | LCC JA70 (ebook) | DDC
320.9--dc23/eng/20221101
LC record available at https://lccn.loc.gov/2022038395
LC ebook record available at https://lccn.loc.gov/2022038396

5482 Argosy Avenue
Huntington Beach, CA 92649
www.tcmpub.com
ISBN 978-1-0876-9522-8

Table of Contents

Leaders for the People....................4

The Evolution of Government 6

Modern Government 10

Mass Communication....................14

Governments Working Together..........18

Civic Involvement 22

Evolving for the Future..................26

Map It! 28

Glossary 30

Index..................................31

Learn More!............................32

Leaders for the People

Humans have always looked to leaders to guide them. Long ago, as families grew into villages, they chose **tribal** leaders. This was how the seeds of the first governments began.

Today, every country has a government. There are also local governments for cities and states. Government leaders protect and care for their lands. They create rules and laws. They protect their people, too. Governments provide services for people. These may include education and **health care**. Providing government services costs money. Most countries require their people to pay **taxes**. These funds help pay for projects and services.

There are many types of government leaders. Let's explore the systems of government around the world!

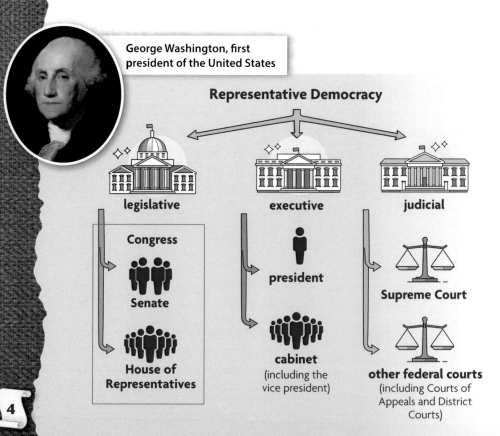

George Washington, first president of the United States

Representative Democracy

legislative

executive

judicial

Congress

president

Senate

Supreme Court

House of Representatives

cabinet
(including the vice president)

other federal courts
(including Courts of Appeals and District Courts)

Types of Governments

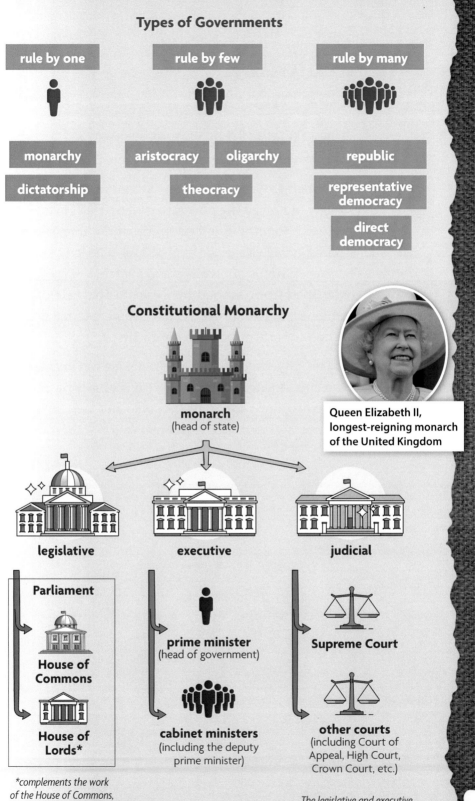

rule by one	rule by few	rule by many
monarchy	aristocracy / oligarchy	republic
dictatorship	theocracy	representative democracy
		direct democracy

Constitutional Monarchy

monarch
(head of state)

Queen Elizabeth II, longest-reigning monarch of the United Kingdom

legislative

executive

judicial

Parliament

House of Commons

House of Lords*

prime minister
(head of government)

cabinet ministers
(including the deputy prime minister)

Supreme Court

other courts
(including Court of Appeal, High Court, Crown Court, etc.)

*complements the work of the House of Commons, but is independent from it

The legislative and executive branches are closely entwined.

The Evolution of Government

Since ancient times, governments have evolved. Governments change as the world and its people change.

Many ancient cities were city-states. Athens in Greece was a city-state. A city-state had the power to govern itself. In many ways, it acted like a country. But it covered just the area of the city and its surrounding villages or farms. Over time, city-states formed their own systems of currency and militaries. City-states were far apart from one another. And it could take days to travel from one city to another. So if a city were to fall under attack, it needed to form an army to defend itself.

In some cases, city-states had kings. Each king was in charge of running the city. A king is a royal title that is usually passed from a father to his oldest son. Queens could also rule. In other city-states, aristocrats ruled. These people were members of the upper class.

the Parthenon in Athens, Greece

Prince's Palace of Monaco

Some city-states still exist. Singapore is one of them. It is an island in Southeast Asia. It was once part of Malaysia. But it separated into its own city-state in 1965. Other current city-states are Monaco and Vatican City.

The Oldest Government

The oldest known civilization with a government was Sumer. It was located near modern-day Iraq. It was first settled between 4500 and 4000 BCE. Near the end of this civilization, the oldest existing lawbook was written. It is a clay tablet called the *Code of Ur-Nammu*. The laws in this book were written to bring justice to the kingdom.

Senate meeting in Rome

Around 509 BCE, the king of Rome was overthrown. In his place, Rome established a republic. Kings and emperors did not rule in the republic. Instead, leaders were chosen by the people. These leaders were called *consuls*. The consuls appointed senators. Roman men met at assemblies. At these assemblies, everyone discussed issues. They voted as a group to make new laws or decisions. Senators could advise them.

North America was another place where people met in groups to make important decisions. To stop war between tribes in the Northeast, American Indians formed a **council** of chiefs. The council decided on issues that affected the tribes. Their conversations led to peace. Tribes around North America began to meet in councils.

Dakota Indian Council, 1847

Modern-Day Councils

Countries around the world have their own types of councils. Some councils might be known as congresses. **Parliaments**, senates, and assemblies are also types of councils. These are all groups of people who meet to discuss and vote on laws.

A constitution is a document that explains a country's government and laws. It explains how power is distributed. It also explains the rights people have. And it provides guidance for councils to write new laws. New constitutions can be written as a country changes over time. They can also be edited. Amendments are edits to a constitution. They are used to update the document. Every country has some sort of constitution.

House of Commons in London

Seating Arrangements

Most legislative buildings have rooms that are built for lawmaking discussions. In the U.S. Senate, the seats are set in a semi-circle. The person speaking goes to the front and center. In Canada and the United Kingdom, the seats are set in two rectangular rows with an aisle between them. The person speaking goes to one end of the aisle.

Modern Government

There are many different types of governments. Each one is unique. Some countries even have a mixture of government styles. And governments can share certain qualities. These are just a few of the most common types of governments.

Democracy

Democracies can be found around the world. In this type of government, power is given to the people. They make choices about their leaders. They choose who to vote for. There are two types of democracies: direct democracy and representative democracy. In a direct democracy, the people discuss issues. They make laws together. Representative democracies are more common today. People vote to elect officials. The officials then discuss issues and make laws. The United States, Mexico, South Africa, and many other countries have democracies.

people voting in South Africa

Small but Mighty

Some types of governments do not have many leaders. In an aristocracy, the leaders are a small group of people. They are specifically chosen because they are highly qualified. In an oligarchy, just a few people are in charge. A small group of people leads and makes laws. A plutocracy can be considered a type of oligarchy. In a plutocracy, only very wealthy people are in charge.

King Salman of Saudi Arabia

Communism

Communism is a political theory. In a communist
government, common things are shared. They are owned by
everyone. Individual people can own their own houses. But
they cannot own factories. They cannot own anything that
helps them produce goods. Those things are meant to be
shared. The goal is to try to make the sharing of wealth fair for
everyone. **Socialism** also ties into this idea. The Soviet Union's
Communist Party followed communist ideas. But it never fully
achieved communism. Today, no governments are strictly
communist. Cuba and China have communist parties.

Dictatorship

In a dictatorship, one person has all the
power. They are not limited. Dictators
sometimes use violence or force to show their
power. People who live under this type of
government may have limited freedoms. For
example, they may not have freedom of speech.
The German government in the 1930s was a
dictatorship.

North Korean supreme
leader Kim Jong-un

Local Government

The community where you live has its own local government. A city government is often run by a mayor and a council. They make decisions that only affect that city. A city government reports to a larger government. This might be a **district** or a **county**. A county is made up of several cities or towns. Most counties are run by a council. Each council has a leader. The county provides services for the people living there. It can collect taxes for these services. Multiple counties combined can make a state. This is true in the United States and Mexico. In Canada, these combined counties are known as provinces.

Monarchy

Kings and queens are the leaders of monarchies. In this type of government, the monarch is the leader of a country for life. Typically, their reign is **hereditary**. This means that when a king or queen dies, their son or daughter becomes the monarch. Several countries in Europe have monarchies. The United Kingdom and its royal family are well-known. Countries such as Spain, Denmark, and Belgium have royal families, too. Some

Queen Margrethe II of Denmark

countries have elected monarchies. A small group of people votes on who will be the monarch. This happens in Malaysia and in Cambodia.

Theocracy

A theocracy is tied to a religion. The religious leaders hold positions of power in government. Laws may be based on the beliefs in that religion. This type of government was more common in the past, but it still exists. Vatican City is one example.

Senate meeting in Canada

Constitutional Monarchy

In constitutional monarchies, an elected government makes laws. The monarch does not have direct involvement. They do not have a say in the lawmaking process. Canada's government is an example of this. The monarch of the United Kingdom is the monarch of Canada. It is part of the Commonwealth of Nations. This refers to countries that used to be part of the British Empire.

Mass Communication

No invention may have been more important to governments than the printing press. Books were once made by hand. They were expensive to make. Only wealthy people could afford books. Printing presses changed that. Books became easier, cheaper, and faster to make. They were now available to everyone.

Soon, daily newspapers were printed. More people learned how to read. The public became informed about current events. They could read about new laws. New ideas about governments spread across Europe and then to North America.

Printing presses caused change in other ways, too. **Revolutions** started. Governments **toppled**. An informed public made all the difference.

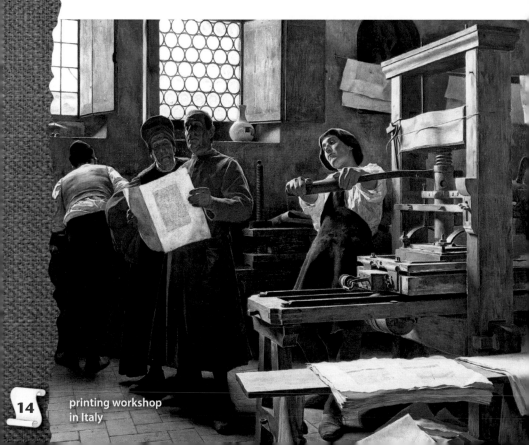

printing workshop in Italy

A family listens to the radio in England in 1942.

Technology developed more over time. The first radio broadcast took place in 1920. It was Election Day in the United States. The station wanted to broadcast election results before the newspapers did. It wanted to show the world how fast news can travel with radios. After that, radios became very popular. They were a constant news source. Families would gather and listen to them.

During World War II, radios were used around the world to entertain and inform the public. Leaders knew how important radios were. They could reach many people. Leaders began to give speeches on the radio. People could hear what their leaders sounded like. Before, they could only read their speeches in newspapers.

The Printing Press

models of Bi Sheng's printing tables

The first printing press is believed to have been invented in China. The oldest block-printed book in China was printed in 868 CE. In 1045, Bi Sheng invented movable type. This meant that each letter or character had its own piece. In 1297, Wang Zhen improved the invention with mechanics. This made the system of printing faster. Over time, more improvements were made. The concept of the printing press spread to other cultures.

People debate in ancient Greece.

Debates are a big part of government. A debate takes place when people with different views discuss a topic. It takes skill and knowledge to debate. In government, politicians debate one another. Many countries around the world have candidates debate before elections. These debates are important to watch. Each candidate wants to show they are the right person to lead the country.

The first televised presidential debate in the United States was in 1960. It was between John F. Kennedy and Richard Nixon. Before this, debates were only on the radio. Or people could read about them in the newspaper. With the debate on TV, people could see it themselves. People who heard the debate on the radio said Nixon won. But people who watched on TV said Kennedy won.

Why was there a difference? Nixon's makeup for the cameras was not put on well. The studio lights made him sweat. His suit caused him to look pale. After the debate, Nixon's mother called him to ask if he was sick. In contrast, Kennedy appeared confident. He seemed more put together than Nixon. How a potential leader appeared began to matter in ways it had not before.

This idea has grown over time. Media can be used to appeal to the masses. This is why fact-checkers have become important in debates and news articles. Fact-checkers are neutral. They do not choose sides. They only report what is true or false.

The Internet and Elections

A lot of money was spent on political ads during the 2020 U.S. elections. In total, $8.5 billion was spent. About 18 percent was spent on digital media. Examples of digital media include Google™, Instagram™, and YouTube™ ads. This was a huge change from previous elections. In 2016, only two to three percent of advertising money was spent on digital media.

Governments Working Together

Countries have relationships with one another. The leaders in some countries get along. They collaborate to solve problems. Other leaders do not work together. One example of an issue countries can work on together is trade. It takes a lot of teamwork to trade goods in an efficient way. So, how do they work together?

Governments use diplomats. Diplomats are people who are experts in working with governments. They help keep relationships on good terms. Diplomats work in each country around the world. They represent their home countries in **negotiations**. Diplomats work with other governments to ensure peace. They can help solve problems that arise and write treaties. A treaty is an agreement between two or more countries. For example, a treaty brought an end to World War I. Two treaties formed the European Union. This is an organization of European countries that helps with trade and other issues.

THE
TREATY OF PEACE
BETWEEN
THE ALLIED AND ASSOCIATED POWERS
AND
GERMANY,
The Protocol annexed thereto, the Agreement respecting the military occupation of the territories of the Rhine,
AND THE
TREATY
BETWEEN
FRANCE AND GREAT BRITAIN
RESPECTING
Assistance to France in the event of unprovoked aggression by Germany.
Signed at Versailles, June 28th, 1919.

signing of the Treaty of Versailles, 1919

G20 OSAKA SUMMIT 2019

Government leaders and diplomats have a meeting to discuss issues.

Many people who want to be diplomats study political science in college. They learn about governments. They learn about the different types and levels of government. Diplomats also learn how to help people work together well. Their job requires them to deal with global cultures. Sometimes, they learn other languages. Communication skills are key for this job. Diplomats have to communicate well with people from around the world.

Sister Cities

To help promote goodwill, some cities have sister cities or twin towns in other countries. This practice began after World War II. Cities that were heavily affected began helping each other. This practice continues today. Diplomats from sister cities around the world visit and help one another.

Dull, Scotland, is paired with Boring, Oregon.

Ambassadors are high-ranking diplomats. They are chosen by their national leaders. An ambassador's job is to represent their national leader and their country. They live and work in countries away from their home countries. This makes it easier to work with foreign governments. They maintain the relationships between their home countries and the countries where they work.

Benjamin Franklin was the first American ambassador to work with a foreign government.

Each ambassador lives and works in an **embassy**. Embassies belong to their home countries. For example, Mexico's embassy in Dublin belongs to Mexico. When you enter the embassy, you are entering Mexican territory.

Embassy of Mexico in Dublin, Ireland

The UN Security Council meets in New York City.

The United Nations (UN) is a global organization. The UN formed after World War II. It has a council called the *General Assembly*. The assembly has members from 193 countries. The UN does not have the power to create laws. But it does help make the world safe for everyone. It helps to keep peace. Members of the UN work as diplomats. They help create treaties among countries. They also write **resolutions**. These explain the UN's views on global matters. The resolutions are meant to be viewed as guidance for the governments of countries around the world. The UN meets every year. If emergencies come up, they can have special sessions. The headquarters are located in New York City.

International Organizations

Governments work together in many ways. Countries around the world can take part in organizations. The World Trade Organization is one example. It creates rules for trade among countries. The International Monetary Fund is another. It helps with trade, too. But it mostly works to help countries with economic growth.

Civic Involvement

Members of a country are called *citizens*. The citizens of a country are protected by their government. It is not easy to become a citizen of a new country. Countries have their own rules about how to become a citizen. This can be a long process.

One way people become a citizen of a country is to be born there. In some countries, it is easier to become a citizen if at least one of your parents is already a citizen. Some countries allow you to become a citizen if you marry someone who is a citizen. But most countries have other, more difficult requirements. You may even need to take a long test about citizenship and what it means to be a citizen of that country.

New Canadian citizens are sworn in.

National Anthem of South Africa

The national anthem of South Africa has five languages in it. They are five of the most commonly spoken languages in South Africa: Xhosa, Zulu, Sethotho, Afrikaans, and English. Regardless of a person's native language, they are supposed to sing in all five languages.

For example, there are several rules to become a citizen of Thailand. First, you have to live there for at least five years. Being able to write, speak, and understand the Thai language is required. You cannot have a criminal record. You must have a job in Thailand. And you will have to sing the national anthem of Thailand.

It is also possible to have **dual** citizenship. This occurs when you are the citizen of two or more countries. But not every country allows dual citizenship. Applying to be a citizen of another country comes with a risk. You may lose citizenship in your home country.

Grand Palace in Bangkok, Thailand

A citizen has an **obligation** to their country. For example, a citizen may have to pay taxes. They might also have to join the military. In Brazil, men must join the military after their 18th birthdays. In Sweden, both men and women can be **drafted** into the military. Many countries have some type of draft. A draft is also known as **conscription**.

Another common obligation is voting during elections. Different countries have different laws about voting. Brazil and some other countries allow a citizen to vote when they have turned 16. In the United States, a person can vote when they have turned 18. In most countries, voting is optional. In 22 countries, people must vote. If they do not vote, they can be fined. Countries make strict rules about who can vote. Some laws ban certain people from voting. For example, criminals cannot vote in some countries.

Obeying the law is part of living in a country. It is part of visiting that country, too! If a person breaks the law, the government can restrict the person's rights. This includes giving fines. In some cases, people can be put in prison.

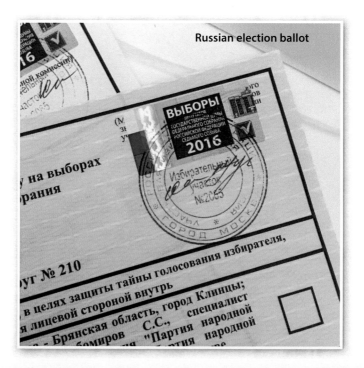
Russian election ballot

People line up to vote in Australia.

A woman votes in Kenya.

Mark of Voting

Some countries have practices in place to stop voter fraud. In India, Afghanistan, and Iraq, people's fingers are marked after they vote. The ink can be purple or black. In some cases, it can stay on their fingers for days or weeks. This prevents them from voting multiple times. Showing their fingers on Election Day has become a sign of voter pride.

Evolving for the Future

There are many types of governments. An oligarchy is controlled by a small group of people. A monarchy is ruled by a king or queen. A plutocracy is ruled by the wealthy. A theocracy is ruled by religious leaders. A republic is governed by elected leaders. A dictatorship has one leader who keeps control. In a democracy, the people hold the power. And there are even more types of government!

Governments are not perfect systems. They are works in progress. They evolve over time. With the internet, television, and phones, change can happen quickly. Some people have new ideas for the future. They see problems in the world, and they have solutions. Some people participate in their governments and speak up about these issues. Others **protest**, regardless of the consequences.

Governments are run by people. These people come in all ages, sizes, races, and cultures. As the first people realized a long time ago, we are all stronger together. People helping others creates a sense of community. Governments are how it all stays organized.

Supreme Court justices, such as Ketanji Brown Jackson, work in the U.S. government.

New York local government members sign legislation.

Tunisians march in Washington, DC.

Protesting for Change

In December 2010, people in Tunisia protested against the government. They were unhappy with the government's actions. They were also unhappy with the president. Many people wanted him to resign. They protested for weeks. They kept protesting until the president had to flee the country. The success of this protest inspired people around the world.

Map It!

Governments conduct their business in special buildings. There are probably a few government buildings in your community. Or there are buildings that have been funded by the government. Think about these government buildings, and create a map to show their locations.

1. Draw a map of the area where you live.

2. On your map, label and include all the government buildings in your community. Consider including the following buildings:
   - city hall
   - police department
   - schools
   - local libraries
   - legislative or judicial buildings

3. Share your completed map with a partner.

Montpelier is the capital city of Vermont.

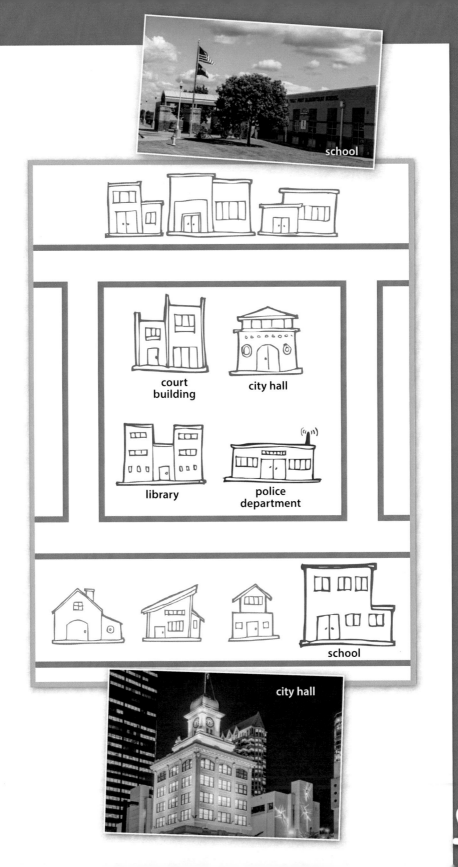

school

court
building

city hall

library

police
department

school

city hall

Glossary

conscription—mandatory enrollment of people especially for military service

council—a group of people who are chosen to make rules, laws, or decisions about something

county—a division of a state or of a country for local government

district—an area or section of a country, city, or town

drafted—enlisted (someone) into the armed services

dual—having two of something

embassy—a building where people work to represent foreign countries

health care—medical care

hereditary—received or passed from a parent to their children, or an ancestor to an heir

negotiations—discussions about something in order to make an agreement

obligation—something (such as a law, rule, or promise) that requires someone to do something

parliaments—groups of people who are responsible for making the laws in some governments

protest—to show strong disagreement or disapproval of something

resolutions—formal statements of feelings or decisions made by a group

revolutions—movements or attempts to overthrow current governments and start new ones

socialism—social system in which factories or things used to produce goods are owned by the government and the government distributes goods

taxes—amounts of money that governments require people to pay according to their incomes, the value of their properties, etc. and that is used to pay for things done by the government

toppled—fell or became overthrown

tribal—belonging to a group of people, such as families and relatives, who have the same language, customs, and beliefs

Canada-U.S. border

Canada Border Services Agency

Agence des services frontaliers du Canada

Pacific Highway Port of Entry

Autoroute du Pacifique Port d'entrée

Canada

Index

Australia, 25

Belgium, 12

Brazil, 24

Cambodia, 12

Canada, 9, 12–13, 22

China, 11, 15

Code of Ur-Nammu, 7

Cuba, 11

Denmark, 12

Elizabeth II, 5

Greece, 6, 16

India, 25

Iraq, 7, 25

Kenya, 25

Malaysia, 7, 12

Mexico, 10, 12, 20

Monaco, 7

New York City, 21

printing press, 14–15

Rome, 8

Russia, 11, 24

South Africa, 10, 22

Spain, 12

Sumer, 7

Sweden, 24

Thailand, 23

United Nations, 21

United States, 4, 10, 12, 15–17, 24, 26

Vatican City, 7, 12–13

Washington, George, 4

World War I, 18

World War II, 15, 19, 21

Learn More!

Your school is like a small government. To become a citizen, you have to enroll in the school. There are rules you have to obey. There is usually a person in charge, such as a principal or headmaster. They often report to a school board. Some schools even have parent councils.

- With a group, make a graphic organizer to show how your school is organized.

- Think about the following questions as you make your organizer: Who is in charge? What other adults help run the school? What are the various jobs in the school?

- Include the responsibilities of each job on your organizer.

Italian primary school